Englisch-Stars
3
Comics

Erarbeitet von

Barbara Gleich
Irene Reindl
Katrin Schmidt
Britta Schöpe

Illustriert von

Wilfried Poll

Cornelsen

 Comic
16601   16651

New colours for Sally

16602

I look so boring, I'm only brown.

16603

I look so boring, I'm only pink and brown.

16604

16605

16606

I look so boring, I'm only pink, brown and green.

16607

16608

That's great. I'm pink, brown, yellow, blue and green.

16609

Oh no, it's raining. Now I'm all brown again.

16610

3

✏ 1. Draw lines. ☑ ❓

17101   17102   17151

orange
17104

brown
17103

green
17105

17115

yellow
17113

17114

17116

white
17106

black
17112

17124

17117

black
17112

17123

17118

red
17107

pink
17111   17122

17120

17119

purple
17108

blue
17110

grey
17109

17121

✏ 2. Write. ☑

17201

17202

17203

I'm _____

and _____ .

17204

I'm _____

and _____ .

17205

I'm _____

and _____ .

17206

I'm _____

and _____ .

In welchen Farben sind die Gesichter der Kinder geschminkt?

4

3. Correct or wrong? Look, read and tick. ☑

I'm black and brown.

I'm pink, green and brown.

Mache einen Haken bei den Bildern, die richtig sind.

I'm pink, yellow, green and brown.

I'm green, pink, purple, blue and brown.

17603
17604
17605 
17606

4. How do you like Sally best? Colour and write.

Wie gefällt dir Sally am besten? Male sie in deinen Lieblingsfarben an und vervollständige den Satz.

17652

That's great. I'm _____.

5

Comic ?

18101   18151

Who likes lollipops?

18102

We have got **one** bread, **two** bottles of milk and **three** oranges.

Four bananas.

18103

Five apples.

What's that, Billy? **Six** lollipops? No, Billy!

18104

18105

Seven, **eight** rolls.

ROLLS

18106

And a package with **nine** chocolate bars.

CHOCOLATE

18107 Oh no, Billy, not again. **Ten** lollipops?

Please, Mum.

26.30

18108

Wow! Thank you, Billy. I love lollipops.

18109   18110

1. Circle the words and write. ✓

18601

18602

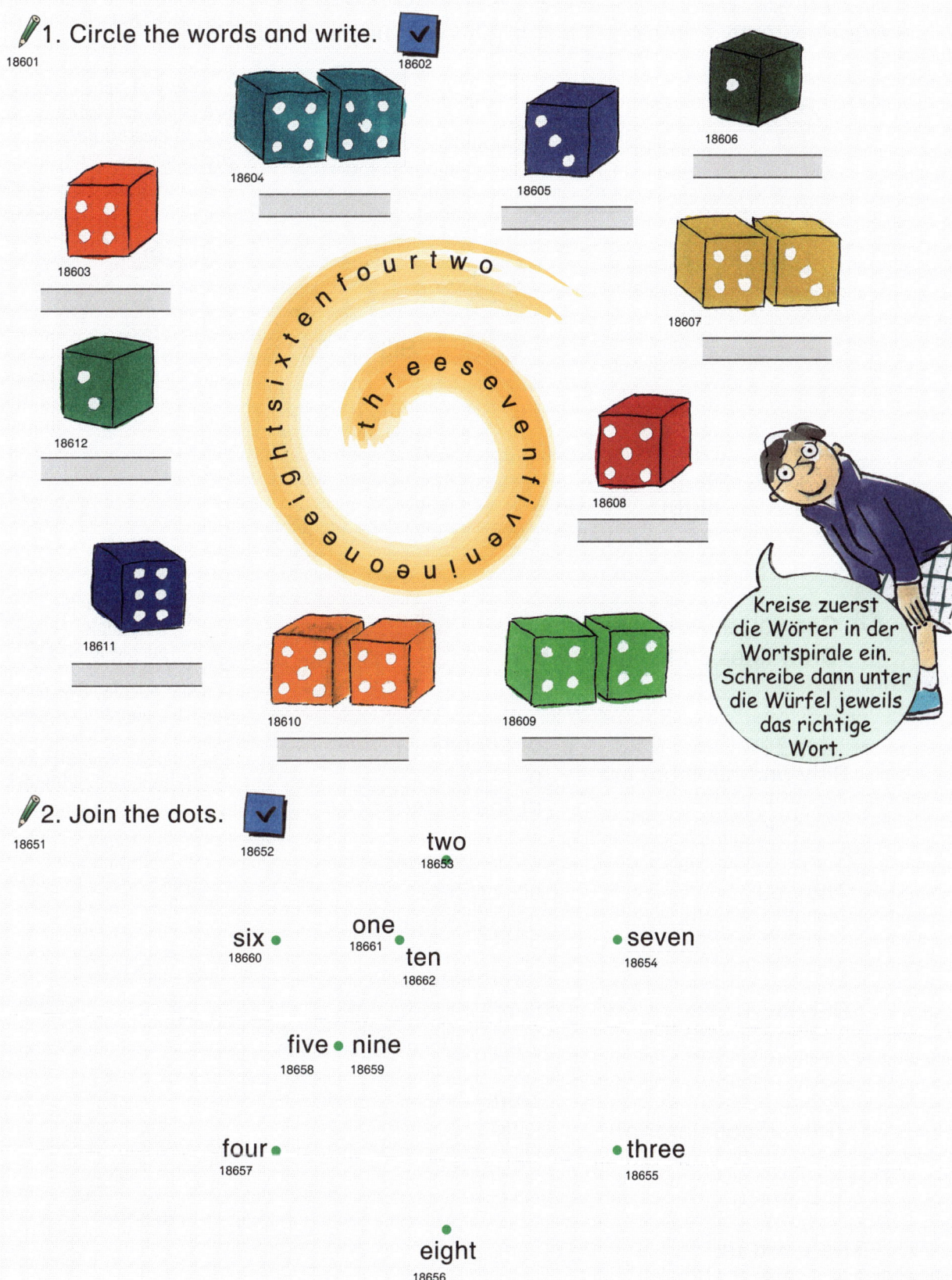

18604 _____

18605 _____

18606 _____

18603 _____

18607 _____

18612 _____

18608 _____

18611 _____

18610 _____

18609 _____

Kreise zuerst die Wörter in der Wortspirale ein. Schreibe dann unter die Würfel jeweils das richtige Wort.

2. Join the dots. ✓

18651

18652

two
18653

six •
18660

one •
18661

• seven
18654

ten
18662

five • nine
18658   18659

four •
18657

• three
18655

•
eight
18656

3. How many of these things do Billy and his mum buy? Write. ✔️

19101

19103   19104   19105   19106

_____   _____   _____   _____

> 19102
> Wie viel der jeweils abgebildeten Sachen kaufen Billy und seine Mutter?

19107   19108   19109

_____   _____   _____   Billy buys _____ .

one	two	three	four
19001	19002	19003	19004
five	eight	nine	ten
19005	19006	19007	19008

4. Can you answer the questions? ✔️
   Draw lines and find the word.
   19152

19151

> One purple, two purple, three purple lollipops,
>
> four purple, five purple, six purple lollipops,
>
> seven purple, eight purple, nine purple lollipops,
>
> ten lollipops for me!

Billy and his mum are	at school. (n) at home. (z) at the supermarket. (f)
They buy	three oranges. (o) six oranges. (i) nine oranges. (e)
Billy buys	ten lollipops. (u) five lollipops. (n) eight lollipops. (r)
The lollipops are for	Mum. (e) Billy. (o) Sally. (r)

The word is: _____

19153

 1. Look and write.

20101 20102 20151

	1	2	3
A	20103	20104	20105
B	20106	20107	20108
C	20109	20110	20111
D	20112	20113	20114

Suche das Feld in der Tabelle und schreibe das richtige Wort in die Zeile

B2 _____   C3 _____

A1 _____   C1 _____

D3 _____   A3 _____

B3 _____   B1 _____

C2 _____   D2 _____

D1 _____   A2 _____

scissors	rubber	schoolbag	pencil case
20001	20002	20003	20004

water colours picture folder
20005   20006   20007

glue book pen ruler pencil
20008 20009 20010 20011 20012

10

2. Find the word and draw. ✓

20601

Entziffere das Wort und male den Gegenstand.

enp	lurer	berbru
20603	20604	20605
eulg	srosciss	cinpel
20606	20607	20608

20602

3. What do Sally and Koala need for their art lesson?
   Tick the correct answers. ✓

20651   20652

- pen   - coloured pencils   - book   - rubber   - ruler
20653   20654   20655   20656   20657

- folder   - water colours   - pencil case   - scissors   - glue
20658   20659   20660   20661   20662

4. Number the pictures in the correct order.
   Draw lines. ✓

20701   20702

Nummeriere die Bilder in der richtigen Reihenfolge. Verbinde dann mit der passenden Sprechblase.

I don't like it.

20703

That's a great picture of my best friend.

20706   20704

Can I have your grey pencil, please?

20705

20707   20708

11

 Comic

21101   21151

A walk at night

21102

Panel 21102 (top left): Let's start our night walk.

Panel (top right): Lilly, are you scared?

Yes, give me your hand.

21103

Panel 21103: Ouch! My head!

21106

Panel 21106: Shhh! What is it? I can see eyes.

Panel 21107: Oh, look at the long ears! It's only a little rabbit.

21105   21106   21107

Panel 21108: My feet hurt.

And I'm really hungry now.

Let's go back.

I'm tired.

Panel 21109: Yummy, sausages!

A great walk. I'm so happy it was only a rabbit.

21108   21109

12

1. Write and draw.

21601

21602

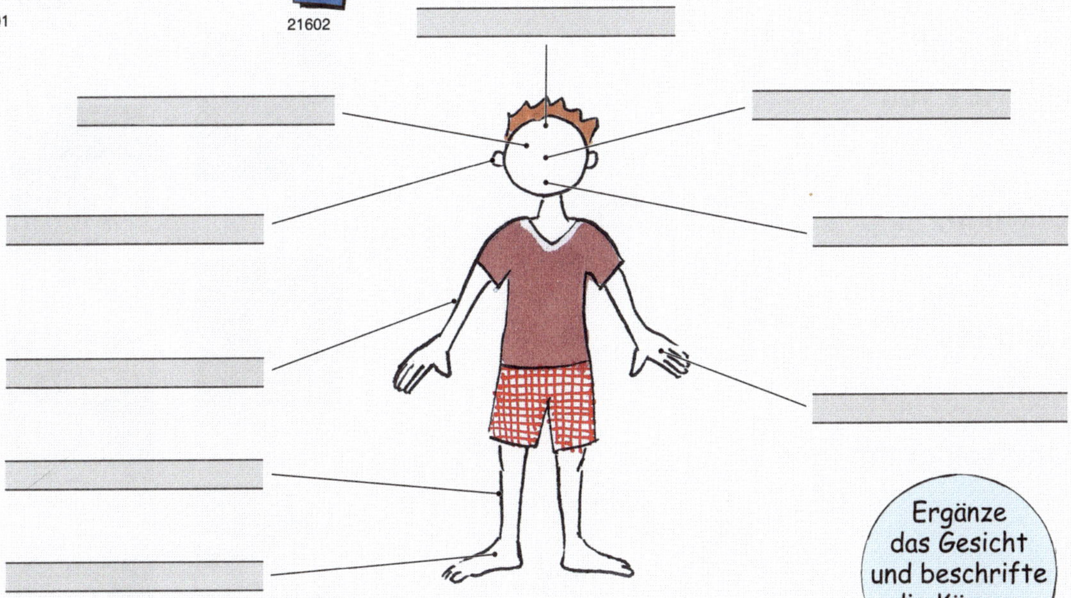

head
21501

eyes
21502

mouth
21503

ears
21504

nose
21505

legs
21506

arms
21507

hands
21508

foot/feet
21509

Ergänze
das Gesicht
und beschrifte
die Körper-
teile.

2. How do they feel? Do the crossword.

21651

21652

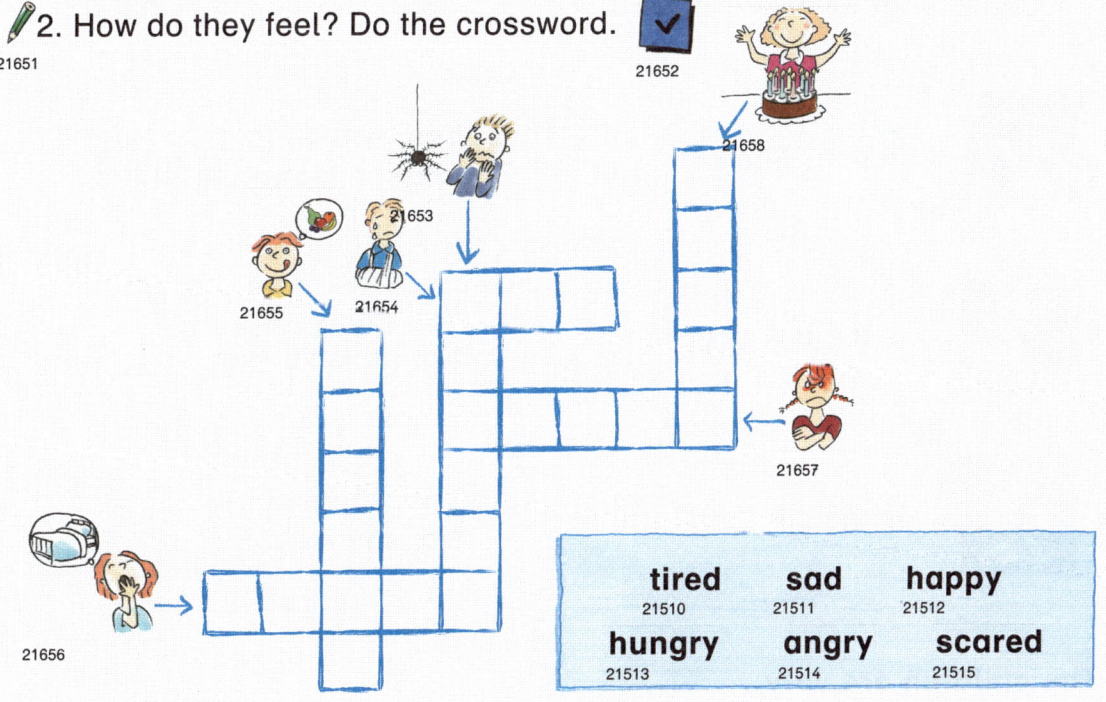

21658

21653

21655

21654

21657

21656

tired
21510

sad
21511

happy
21512

hungry
21513

angry
21514

scared
21515

3. Look at the comic and complete the sentences. Draw lines.

22101

Lilly, are you ⬚⬚⬚⬚⬚⬚⬚⬚⬚?

22102

Ouch! My ⬚⬚⬚⬚⬚⬚⬚⬚⬚!

22103

22104

I can see ⬚⬚⬚⬚⬚⬚⬚⬚.

22105

Oh, look at the long ⬚⬚⬚⬚⬚⬚⬚⬚⬚!

22106

I'm really ⬚⬚⬚⬚⬚⬚⬚ now.

22107

I'm so ⬚⬚⬚⬚⬚⬚⬚ it was only a rabbit.

22108

4. Draw lines and circle the correct letters.
Find out, how the children feel.

22151

22152

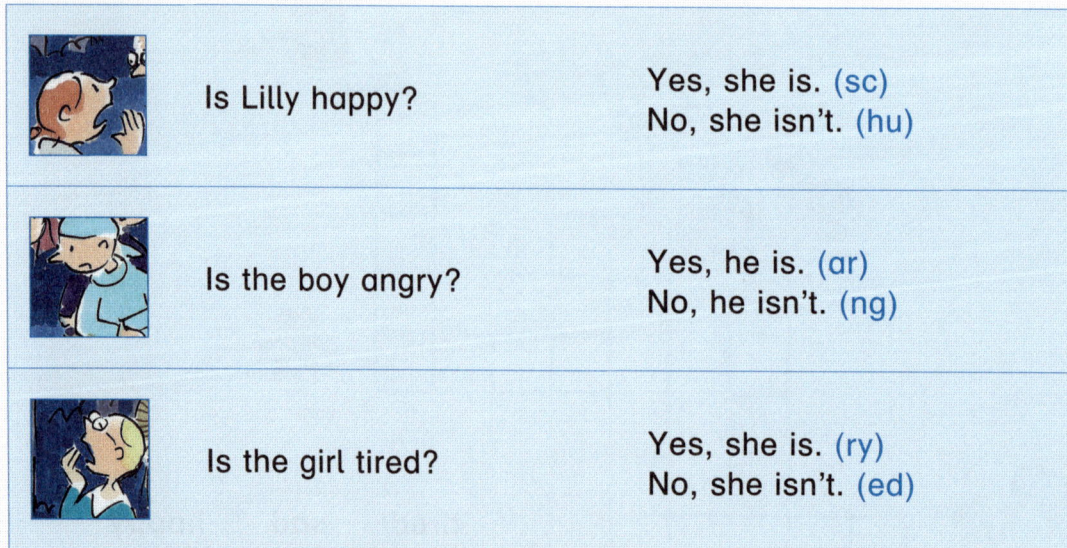

	Is Lilly happy?	Yes, she is. (sc) No, she isn't. (hu)
	Is the boy angry?	Yes, he is. (ar) No, he isn't. (ng)
	Is the girl tired?	Yes, she is. (ry) No, she isn't. (ed)

The children are very ⬚⬚⬚⬚⬚⬚⬚.

Comic
22601
22651

Money for new toys
22602

22603
22604
22605
22606
22607
22608
22609
22610
22611

1. Where are the toys? Look and write.

23101
23102   23151

	1	2	3
A	23103	23104	23105
B			
C	23106	23107	23108
	23109	23110	23111

Schreibe zuerst auf, in welchem Feld sich jeweils der Gegenstand befindet. Trage unten dann die Wörter richtig ein.

In which square...

is the **lorry**?   <u>B1</u>

is the **castle**?   _____

is the **spaceship**?   _____

is the **train**?   _____

is the **ball**?   _____

is the **doll**?   _____

is the **racing car**?   _____

are the **inline skates**?   _____

is the **teddy bear**?   _____

23112
_____

 (doll)

23113
_____

(castle)

23114
_____

23115
_____

23116
_____

23117
_____

23118
_____

23119
_____

23120
_____

🖊 2. Match the sentences with the correct person. Draw lines.

23601

We don't need a new doll and
a new racing car.

23603

Let's do a flea market
and sell some toys.

23604

How much are the castle and
the teddy bear?

23605

You have so many toys.
I'm not buying anything else for you.

23606

How much are the ball and the train?

23607

We need money for the doll and
the racing car.

23608

23602

23609

23610

23611

23612

23613

🖊 3. What's wrong in the pictures? Write.

23651

23652

Schreibe auf was
fehlt und streiche im Bild durch,
was zu viel ist.

23653

The _____ is missing.

23654

The _____ and the

_____ are _____.

23655

The _____ and the

_____ are _____.

📕 Comic   ❓
24101   24151

Sally's patchwork dress

24102

Great! Tina wants me to come to her birthday party.

Birthday party ♥

I don't know what to wear to the party.

24103

The yellow dress is too small, the red skirt is too big and the blue blouse is too old.

24104

I've got an idea!

24105

24106

That looks nice. I like my new dress.

24107

Mummy, can you help me, please?

24108

24109

24110

I'm off to Tina's party now. Thank you, Mummy, you are great.

24111

1. What can you see? Write.
24601

24602

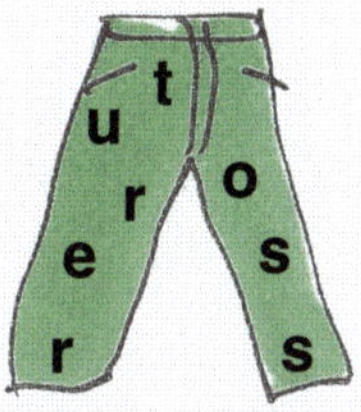

24603

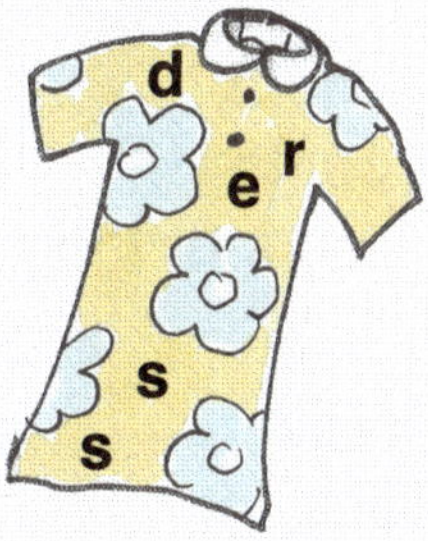

24604

24605

24606

24607

24608

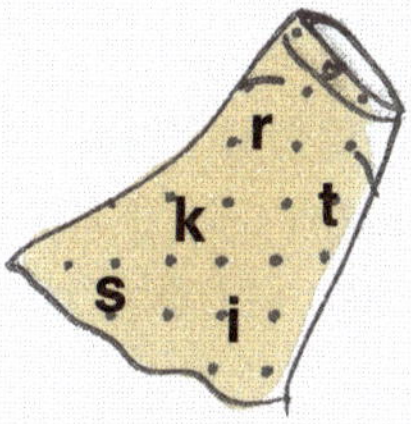

24609

24610

T-shirt	anorak	skirt	pullover	trousers
24501	24502	24503	24504	24505
	blouse	dress	shoes	
	24506	24507	24508	

2. Do the clothes fit? Draw lines and write.
24651

24652

24657

The **pullover** is **too small** .
24653

The **skirt** is **just right** .
24654

The **shoes** are **too big** .
24655

The **blouse** is **too old** .
24656

24658

24659

24660

19

 3. Tick the correct answer.

25101
25102

Sally wants to go	to school.	○
	shopping.	○
	to Tina's birthday party.	○
Sally wants	a dress.	○
	a coat.	○
	a pair of trousers.	○
The red skirt is	too small.	○
	too old.	○
	too big.	○
Sally	likes her new dress.	○
	doesn't like her new dress.	○
	likes her old dress.	○

4. Number the sentences in the correct order. ✔

25151

25152

25153 I don't know what to wear to the party.

25154 I'm off to Tina's party now. Thank you, Mummy, you are great.

25155 Mummy, can you help me, please?

25156 I've got an idea!

25157 The yellow dress is too small, the red skirt is too big and the blue blouse is too old.

25158 Great! Tina wants me to come to her birthday party.

25159 That looks nice. I like my new dress.

25160

20

Comic ?

25601   25651

Rainy holidays

25602

Monday

Holidays from Monday until Sunday – that's fantastic!

It's so foggy today, I hope we will have a sunny week.

25603

Brrr, and it's really cold.

Oh no, it's raining.

Tuesday

Wow, it's so cloudy.

Wednesday

25604

It's rainy and windy. I want to go home.

Me, too.

Thursday

25605   25606   25607

Friday

Saturday

It's already Friday, our holidays are nearly over and it's still cold and rainy.

Sunday

25608

It wasn't very nice. It was rainy, windy and cold.

25609

Did you have nice holidays? What was the weather like?

25610

Oh, poor you. Here it was sunny and warm from Tuesday until Saturday.

25611

21

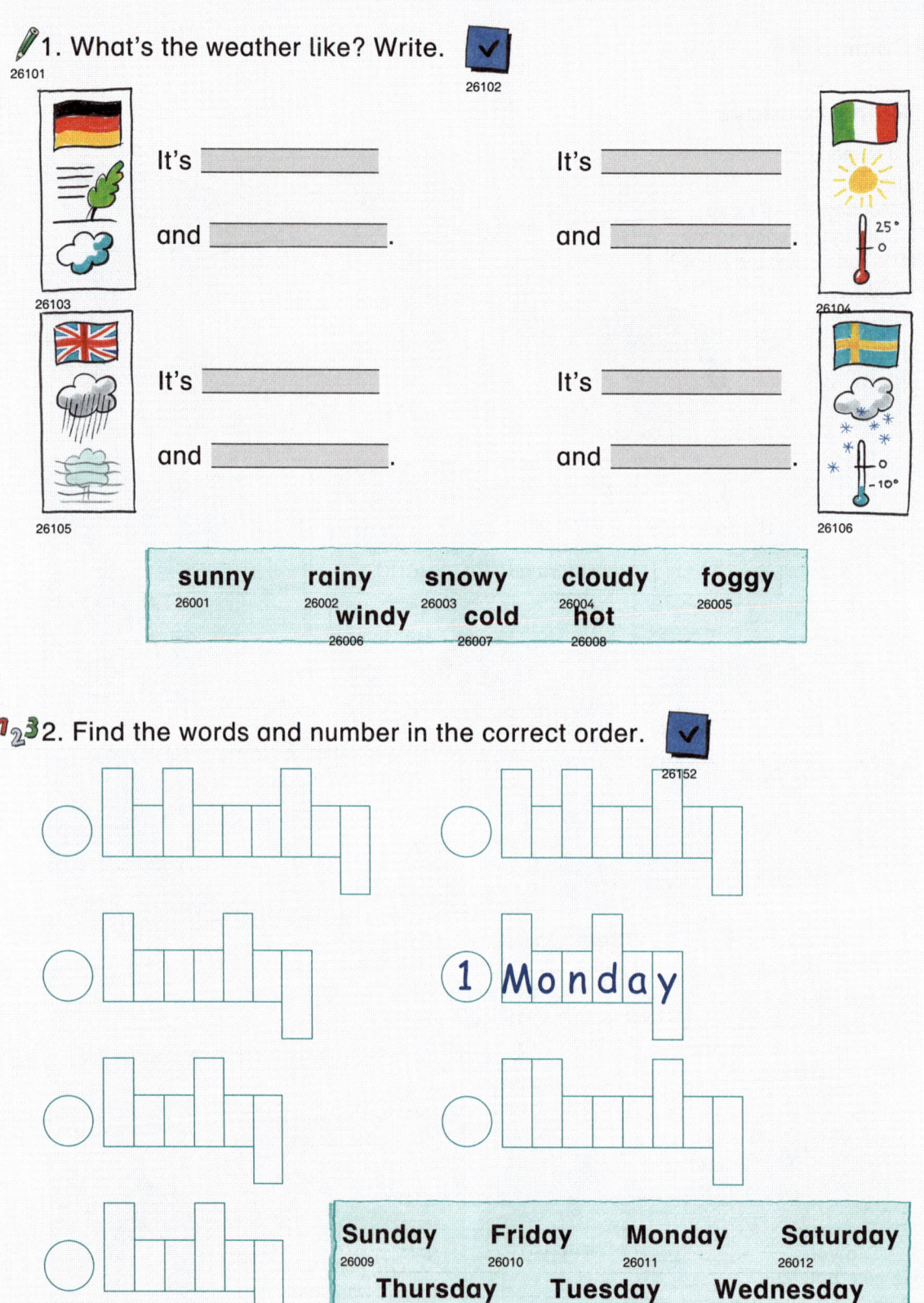

1. What's the weather like? Write. ✔

26101

26102

It's _____

and _____ .

26103

It's _____

and _____ .

26104

It's _____

and _____ .

26105

It's _____

and _____ .

26106

sunny	rainy	snowy	cloudy	foggy
26001	26002	26003	26004	26005

windy   cold   hot

26006   26007   26008

2. Find the words and number in the correct order. ✔

26151

26152

○

○

○

○

○

① Monday

○

Sunday	Friday	Monday	Saturday
26009	26010	26011	26012

Thursday   Tuesday   Wednesday

26013   26014   26015

123 3. Number the pictures in the correct order. Find the word.

26601

YS

> Nummeriere die Bilder in der richtigen Reihenfolge. Die Buchstaben ergeben dann das Lösungswort.

DA

HO

LI

 **from Monday until Sunday!**

4. A postcard from Tim and Kate's holidays. Cross out. 26652

26651

> Streiche die jeweils falsche Aussage durch.

Dear Grandma and Grandpa

Greetings from Rainy Island.
Today is Thursday Friday
and we are going to the zoo.
It's so cold hot here.
The weather is really bad
good.
It's snowy rainy and cloudy
sunny and really windy foggy.
See you on Sunday Friday!

Love, Tim and Kate

📕 Comic ❓
27101   27151

Pool party
27102

Koala, come to our pool party. My whole family will be there.

These are my father, my mother, my brother and my sister.

27103

These are my uncle, my aunt, my cousin, my grandpa and my grandma.

And this is my best friend Koala.

27106

Now let's go swimming in the pool.

27107

27108

SPLASH!

27109

But who is who now? Sally, where are you?

Informationen für Eltern und Lehrkräfte

Englisch-Spaß mit Comic-Stars

Aufbau und Gestaltung der Comic-Stars

Comics haben einen hohen Motivationsgrad. Sie erleichtern das Lesen, da sich der Inhalt durch die Bebilderung einfacher erschließen lässt. Die Comic-Stars führen die Kinder zum ersten Lesen in der Fremdsprache heran und zeigen ihnen, wie viel sie schon selbstständig lesen und verstehen können.

Unterteilt in verschiedene Themenbereiche, können diese unabhängig voneinander gelesen und bearbeitet werden. Jedes Kapitel beginnt mit dem Comic. Daran schließen sich zwei Übungsseiten an. Die erste Seite dient zur Wortschatzwiederholung und -sicherung, während sich die zweite Seite auf den Comic selbst bezieht wobei das Leseverstehen überprüft und der Inhalt reflektiert wird. Die Abschlussseite greift alle Themen nochmals auf und animiert die Kinder dazu sich ein weiteres Mal mit den Comics zu beschäftigen. Eindeutige Aufgabenstellungen und Selbstkontrolle durch den Lösungsteil ermöglichen den Kindern eigenständig mit den Comic-Stars zu arbeiten.

Die beiden deutschsprachigen Kinder Anna und Felix unterstützen mit Tipps und Hilfestellungen.

Für jeden gelesenen Comic und für jeden bearbeiteten und kontrollierten Übungsteil dürfen sich die Kinder mit einem Sternchen-Aufkleber belohnen. Für die letzte Seite gibt es zwei weitere Sterne. Als besonderen Anreiz ergeben die Sterne am Ende des Heftes ein Gesamtbild.

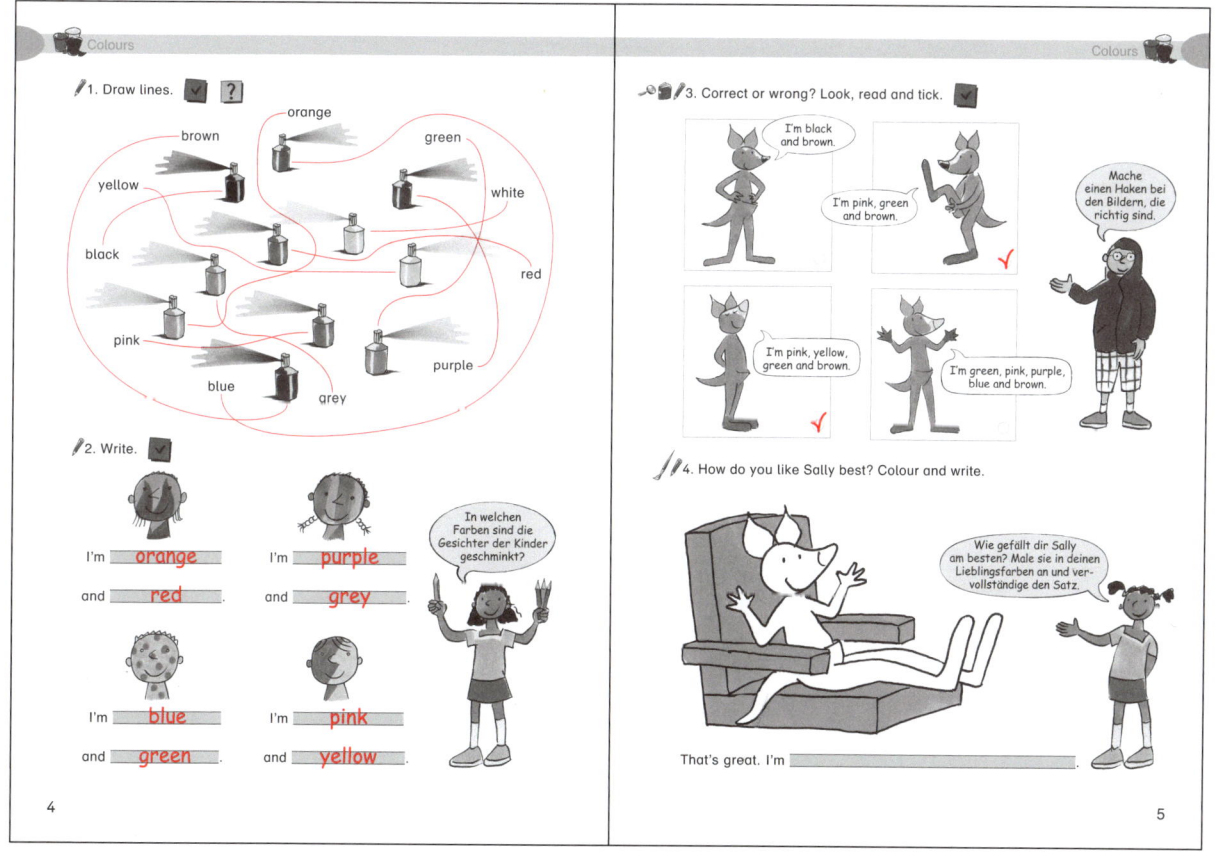

Lösungen

Comic ?

Who likes lollipops?

We have got **one** bread, **two** bottles of milk and **three** oranges.

Four bananas.

Five apples.

What's that, Billy? **Six** lollipops? No, Billy!

Seven, eight rolls.

ROLLS

And a package with **nine** chocolate bars.

CHOCOLATE

Oh no, Billy, not again. **Ten** lollipops?

26.30

Please, Mum.

Wow! Thank you, Billy. I love lollipops.

6

1. Circle the words and write. ✓

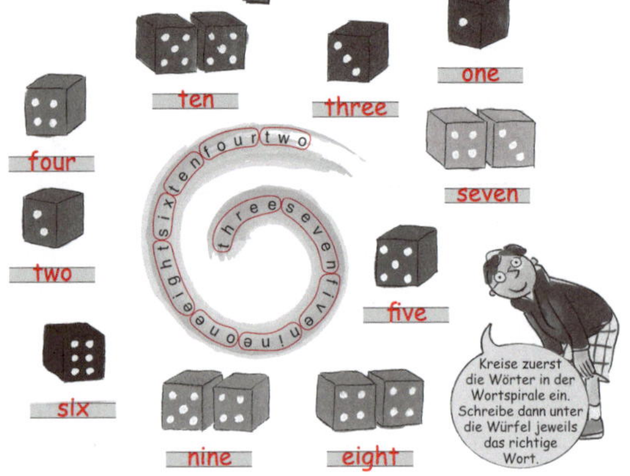

ten   three   one

four   seven

two   five

six   nine   eight

Kreise zuerst die Wörter in der Wortspirale ein. Schreibe dann unter die Würfel jeweils das richtige Wort.

(spiral: three seven ten four two six ten nine one eight)

2. Join the dots. ✓

two
six • one • seven
ten
five • nine
four • • three
eight

7

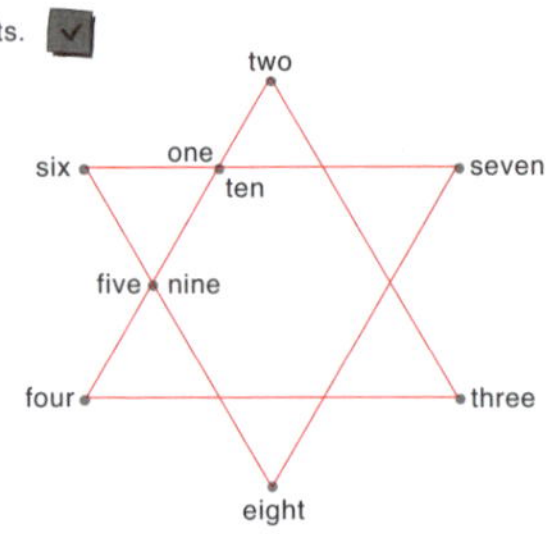

3. How many of these things do Billy and his mum buy? Write. ✓

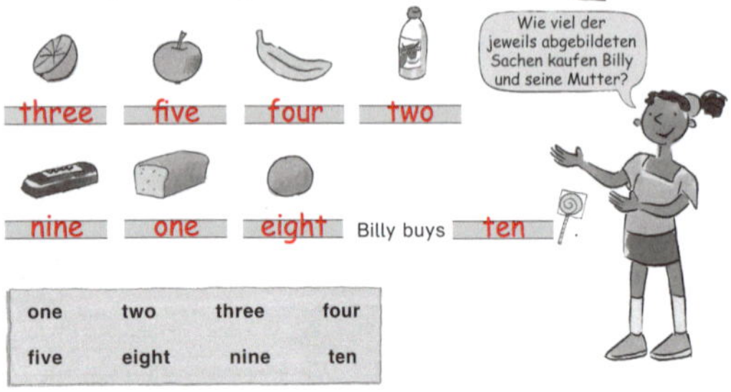

Wie viel der jeweils abgebildeten Sachen kaufen Billy und seine Mutter?

three   five   four   two

nine   one   eight   Billy buys   ten

one	two	three	four
five	eight	nine	ten

4. Can you answer the questions? ✓
Draw lines and find the word.

One purple, two purple, three purple lollipops,

four purple, five purple, six purple lollipops,

seven purple, eight purple, nine purple lollipops,

ten lollipops for me!

	at school. (n)
Billy and his mum are	at home. (z)
	at the supermarket. (f)
	three oranges. (o)
They buy	six oranges. (i)
	nine oranges. (e)
	ten lollipops. (u)
Billy buys	five lollipops. (n)
	eight lollipops. (r)
	Mum. (e)
The lollipops are for	Billy. (o)
	Sally. (r)

The word is: four

8

Comic ?

An art lesson

Make an art work of your best friend. Use your coloured pencils, rubber, ruler, glue, water colours and scissors.

coloured pencils   glue
ruler   scissors   water colours
rubber

That's great. I love art lessons.

Can I have your grey pencil, please?

I don't like it.

Can I have your glue, please?

We need more grey paint.

I've got an idea!

That's a great picture of my best friend.

9

1. Look and write.

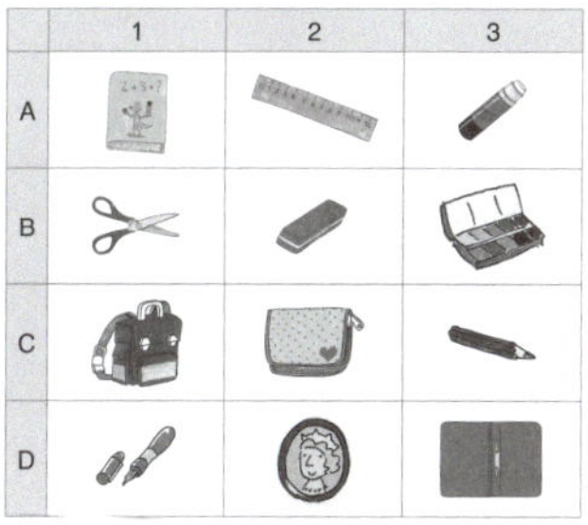

Suche das Feld in der Tabelle und schreibe das richtige Wort in die Zeile

	1	2	3
A			
B			
C			
D			

B2 **rubber**   C3 **pencil**
A1 **book**   C1 **schoolbag**
D3 **folder**   A3 **glue**
B3 **water colours**   B1 **scissors**
C2 **pencil case**   D2 **picture**
D1 **pen**   A2 **ruler**

scissors   rubber   schoolbag   pencil case
water colours   picture   folder
glue   book   pen   ruler   pencil

2. Find the word and draw.

Entziffere das Wort und male den Gegenstand.

enp	lurer	berbru
Füller	**Lineal**	**Radiergummi**

eulg	srosciss	cinpel
Klebstoff	**Schere**	**Bleistift**

3. What do Sally and Koala need for their art lesson? Tick the correct answers.

○ pen   ✓ coloured pencils   ○ book   ✓ rubber   ✓ ruler
○ folder   ✓ water colours   ○ pencil case   ✓ scissors   ✓ glue

4. Number the pictures in the correct order. Draw lines.

Nummeriere die Bilder in der richtigen Reihenfolge. Verbinde dann mit der passenden Sprechblase.

1 — I don't like it.
That's a great picture of my best friend.
3
2 — Can I have your grey pencil, please?

10   11

Comic

A walk at night

Let's start our night walk.
Lilly, are you scared?
Yes, give me your hand.
Ouch! My head!
Shhh! What is it? I can see eyes.
Oh, look at the long ears! It's only a little rabbit.
My feet hurt.
And I'm really hungry now.
Let's go back.
I'm tired.
Yummy, sausages!
A great walk. I'm so happy it was only a rabbit.

1. Write and draw.

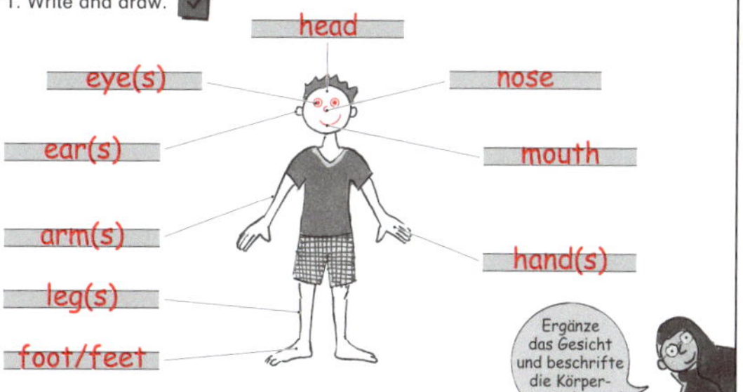

head
eye(s)   **nose**
ear(s)   **mouth**
arm(s)   **hand(s)**
leg(s)
foot/feet

head   eyes   mouth   ears   nose
legs   arms   hands   foot/feet

Ergänze das Gesicht und beschrifte die Körperteile.

2. How do they feel? Do the crossword.

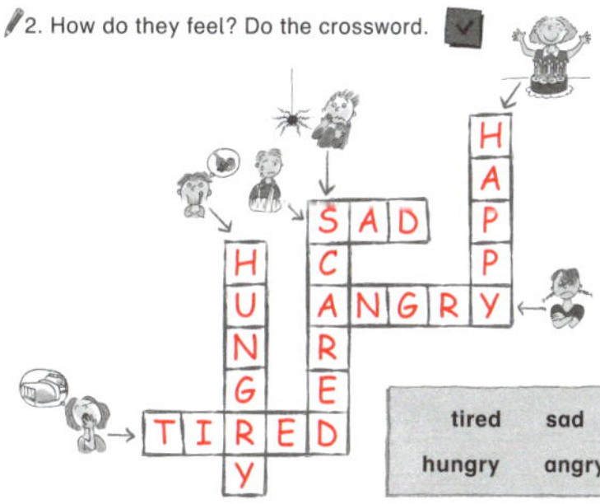

S A D
H A P P Y
H U N G R Y
S C A R E D
A N G R Y
T I R E D

tired   sad   happy
hungry   angry   scared

12   13

Lösungen

3. Look at the comic and complete the sentences. Draw lines. ✓

Lilly, are you **scared**?

Ouch! My **head**!

I can see **eyes**.

Oh, look at the long **ears**!

I'm really **hungry** now.

I'm so **happy** it was only a rabbit.

4. Draw lines and circle the correct letters.
Find out, how the children feel. ✓

	Is Lilly happy?	Yes, she is. (sc) / No, she isn't. (hu)
	Is the boy angry?	Yes, he is. (ar) / No, he isn't. (ng)
	Is the girl tired?	Yes, she is. (ry) / No, she isn't. (ed)

The children are very hungry.

14

Comic ?

Money for new toys

- Mum, I want this doll.
- I want this racing car.
- You have so many toys. I'm not buying anything else for you.
- Let's do a flea market and sell some toys.
- We need money for the doll and the racing car.
- How much are the castle and the teddy bear?
- Oh no, not my castle.
- Oh no, not my teddy bear.
- How much are the ball and the train?
- Oh no, not our ball and train.
- We love our old toys. We don't need a new doll and a new racing car.

15

---

1. Where are the toys? Look and write. ✓ ?

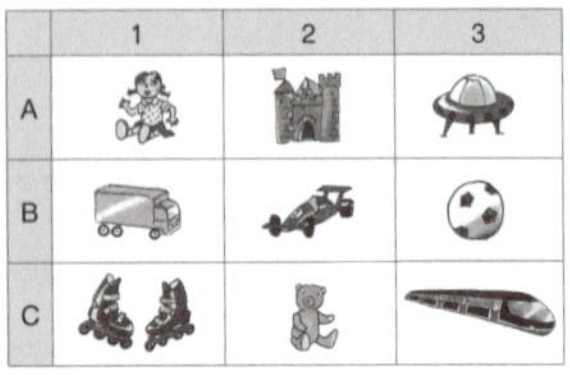

	1	2	3
A			
B			
C			

Schreibe zuerst auf, in welchem Feld sich jeweils der Gegenstand befindet. Trage unten dann die Wörter richtig ein.

In which square...

is the **ball**? **B3**

is the **lorry**? **B1**

is the **doll**? **A1**

is the **castle**? **A2**

is the **racing car**? **B2**

is the **spaceship**? **A3**

are the **inline skates**? **C1**

is the **train**? **C3**

is the **teddy bear**? **C2**

teddy bear   doll   castle

racing car   train   inline skates

ball   spaceship   lorry

16

---

2. Match the sentences with the correct person. Draw lines. ✓

We don't need a new doll and a new racing car.

Let's do a flea market and sell some toys.

How much are the castle and the teddy bear?

You have so many toys. I'm not buying anything else for you.

How much are the ball and the train?

We need money for the doll and the racing car.

3. What's wrong in the pictures? Write. ✓

Schreibe auf was fehlt und streiche im Bild durch, was zu viel ist.

The **doll** is missing.

The **ball** and the **train** are **missing**.

The **castle** and the **teddy bear** are **missing**.

17

Clothes

Comic ?

Sally's patchwork dress

- Great! Tina wants me to come to her birthday party.
- I don't know what to wear to the party.
- The yellow dress is too small, the red skirt is too big and the blue blouse is too old.
- I've got an idea!
- That looks nice. I like my new dress.
- Mummy, can you help me, please?
- I'm off to Tina's party now. Thank you, Mummy, you are great.

18

Clothes

1. What can you see? Write. ✓

trousers
dress
pullover
T-shirt
blouse
shoes
skirt
anorak

| T-shirt | anorak | skirt | pullover | trousers |
| blouse | dress | shoes | | |

2. Do the clothes fit? Draw lines and write. ✓

The pullover is too small .

The skirt is just right .

The shoes are too big .

The blouse is too old .

19

Clothes

3. Tick the correct answer. ✓

Sally wants to go	to school.	
	shopping.	
	to Tina's birthday party.	✓
Sally wants	a dress.	
	a coat.	
	a pair of trousers.	
The red skirt is	too small.	
	too old.	
	too big.	✓
Sally	likes her new dress.	✓
	doesn't like her new dress.	
	likes her old dress.	

1₂34. Number the sentences in the correct order. ✓

2 I don't know what to wear to the party.

7 I'm off to Tina's party now. Thank you, Mummy, you are great.

6 Mummy, can you help me, please?

4 I've got an idea!

3 The yellow dress is too small, the red skirt is too big and the blue blouse is too old.

1 Great! Tina wants me to come to her birthday party.

5 That looks nice. I like my new dress.

20

Weather and days

Comic ?

Rainy holidays

Monday
- Holidays from Monday until Sunday – that's fantastic!
- It's so foggy today, I hope we will have a sunny week.
- Brrr, and it's really cold.
- Oh no, it's raining.

Tuesday
- Wow, it's so cloudy.

Wednesday
- It's rainy and windy. I want to go home.
- Me, too.

Thursday

Friday

Saturday
- It's already Friday, our holidays are nearly over and it's still cold and rainy.

Sunday
- It wasn't very nice. It was rainy, windy and cold.
- Did you have nice holidays? What was the weather like?
- Oh, poor you. Here it was sunny and warm from Tuesday until Saturday.

21

Lösungen

1. What's the weather like? Write. ✓

It's **windy** and **cloudy**.

It's **sunny** and **hot**.

It's **rainy** and **foggy**.

It's **snowy** and **cold**.

sunny	rainy	snowy	cloudy	foggy
windy	cold	hot		

2. Find the words and number in the correct order. ✓

3 **Wednesday**   6 **Saturday**

2 **Tuesday**   1 **Monday**

5 **Friday**   4 **Thursday**

7 **Sunday**

Sunday	Friday	Monday	Saturday
Thursday	Tuesday	Wednesday	

22

3. Number the pictures in the correct order. Find the word. ✓

Nummeriere die Bilder in der richtigen Reihenfolge. Die Buchstaben ergeben dann das Lösungswort.

4 — YS

3 — DA   1 — HO   2 — LI

Holidays from Monday until Sunday!

4. A postcard from Tim and Kate's holidays. Cross out. ✓

Streiche die jeweils falsche Aussage durch.

Dear Grandma and Grandpa

Greetings from Rainy Island.
Today is ~~Thursday~~ Friday
and we are going to the zoo.
It's so ~~cold~~ ~~hot~~ here.
The weather is really bad
~~good~~.
It's ~~snowy~~ rainy and ~~cloudy~~
~~sunny~~ and really windy ~~foggy~~.
See you on Sunday ~~Friday~~!

Love, Tim and Kate

23

📖 Comic ?

Pool party

Koala, come to our pool party. My whole family will be there.

These are my father, my mother, my brother and my sister.

These are my uncle, my aunt, my cousin, my grandpa and my grandma.

And this is my best friend Koala.

Now let's go swimming in the pool.

SPLASH!

But who is who now? Sally, where are you?

24

1. Who is it? Write. ✓

mother   **grandfather**   **father**

brother   **grandmother**   **sister**

aunt   **cousin**   **uncle**

2. Different families. Write. ✓

Schau genau hin und ergänze dann die Sätze.

I live with my father, my **mother** and my **brother**.

I live with my **mother**, my **grandmother** and my **grandfather**.

I live with my **father**, my **mother**, my **sister**, my uncle, my **aunt** and my **cousin**.

25

Family and friends

3. Draw lines.

These are my uncle, my aunt, my cousin, my grandpa and my grandma.

Koala, come to our pool party.

These are my father, my mother, my brother and my sister.

Ordne die Sprechblase dem richtigen Bild zu.

And this is my best friend Koala.

4. Who is it? Read, look and write.

Who is it? He's wearing green trousers.

That's my **uncle**.

Who is it? She's wearing a pink dress.

That's my **mother**.

Who is it? He's wearing a yellow T-shirt.

That's my **grandfather**.

Who is it? She's wearing a purple skirt.

That's my **sister**.

Schau dir den Comic noch mal genau an und ergänze dann die Sätze.

26

Drinks

Comic ?

A game with drinks

Come on, let's play a game.

What is it, Jack?

Ah, that's orange juice.

One is water and one is lemonade.

Ew! That tastes bitter! That's coffee! Now it's your turn!

What is it, Betty?

Yummy, it's my favourite drink, hot chocolate.

Mmmm, one is milk. I like it. The other one is coke.

Now you get my favourite drink.

I'm mixing everything together.

Do you like my special drink?

27

Drinks

1. What is it? Write.

milk **coke** **coffee**

apple juice **orange juice**

hot chocolate **tea**

water **lemonade**

apple juice   milk   coke   lemonade   tea
hot chocolate   coffee   water   orange juice

2. Read and write.

It's cold, bubbly and made from lemons. It's **lemonade**.

It's cold, brown and sweet. Children like it. It's **coke**.

It's cold. It's made from apples. It's **apple juice**.

You can drink it warm or cold. It's white and from a cow.

It's **milk**.

It's hot, brown and sweet. You make it with milk.

It's **hot chocolate**.

28

Drinks

3. Cross out.

Streiche jeweils die falsche Aussage durch.

Jack ~~likes~~ doesn't like coffee.

Coffee tastes bitter ~~sweet~~.

Betty likes ~~doesn't like~~ milk.

Betty's favourite drink is ~~coke~~ hot chocolate.

4. Look at the comic and write.

Schreibe auf, welche Getränke Jack und welche Betty probiert hat.

Jack

orange juice, water, lemonade, coffee

Betty

hot chocolate, milk, coke, special drink

What's your favourite drink?

My favourite drink is

29

Lösungen

Comic ?

Sally's special breakfast

Oh, I'm sooooo tired.

Good morning, Mum.

Good morning, Sally. Would you like milk, orange juice or tea? And would you like a roll with butter or bread with ham?

Just hot chocolate.

Oh, no! I put strawberry jam into the milk.

I'll try it.

Yummy! It's strawberry-jam milk.

Now, I'm ready for school!

Goodbye, Mum. And thank you for the great breakfast.

Oh, Sally!

30

---

1. Find the words and draw lines.

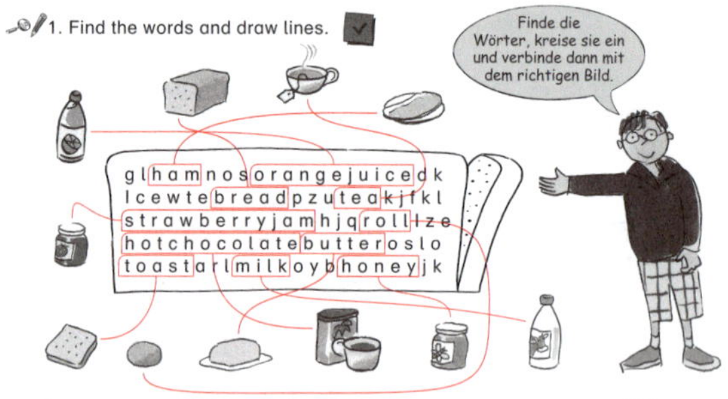

Finde die Wörter, kreise sie ein und verbinde dann mit dem richtigen Bild.

```
g l h a m n o s o r a n g e j u i c e d k
l c e w t e b r e a d p z u t e a k j f k l
s t r a w b e r r y j a m h j q r o l l l z e
h o t c h o c o l a t e b u t t e r o s l o
t o a s t a r l m i l k o y b h o n e y j k
```

2. What do they like for breakfast? Trace the lines and write.

Lucy   Ben   Tom

Lucy likes **tea** and **bread** with **ham**.

Ben likes **orange juice** and **toast** with **butter**.

Tom likes **milk** and a **roll** with **strawberry jam**.

31

---

3. Read and tick the correct answer.

Sally says:	Hello, Mum.	
	Good morning, Mum. ✓	
	Good night, Mum.	
Sally wants …	milk	
	orange juice	for breakfast.
	hot chocolate ✓	
Sally puts …	chocolate	
	strawberry jam ✓	into her milk.
	ham	
Does Sally like strawberry milk?	Yes, she does. ✓	
	No, she doesn't.	

4. Sally's crazy breakfast. Look and write.

On Monday Sally has strawberry-jam milk.

On Tuesday Sally has an **orange-juice roll**.

On Wednesday Sally has **hot-chocolate tea**.

But on Saturday and Sunday, there's no school – and I'm not tired.

On Thursday Sally has **orange-juice milk**.

On Friday Sally has **hot-chocolate bread**.

32

Comic ?

Eating a rainbow

Lucy, eat some fruit. It's good for you.

I don't like to eat what's good for me.

Strawberries are red – and cherries are red, too.

Oranges are orange.

Lemons are yellow – and bananas are yellow, too.

Apples are green – and pears are green, too.

Plums are purple.

Well, grapes are blue.

Good girl, you're eating fruit.

I'm not eating fruit, Mummy, I'm eating a rainbow.

33

Page 34

Fruit

1. Draw lines. ✓

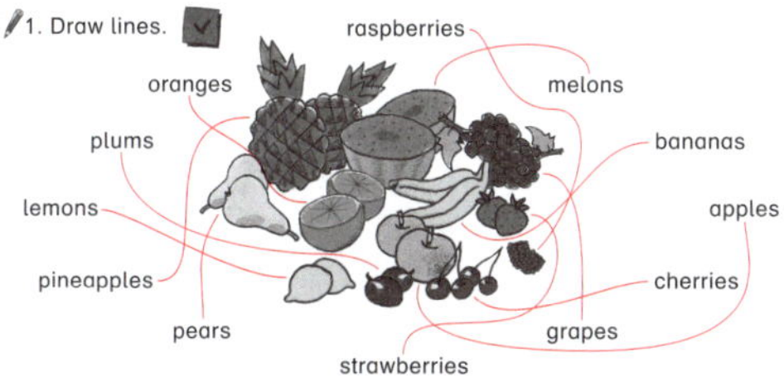

raspberries
oranges
melons
plums
bananas
lemons
apples
pineapples
cherries
pears
grapes
strawberries

2. What can you see in the squares? Write. ✓ ?

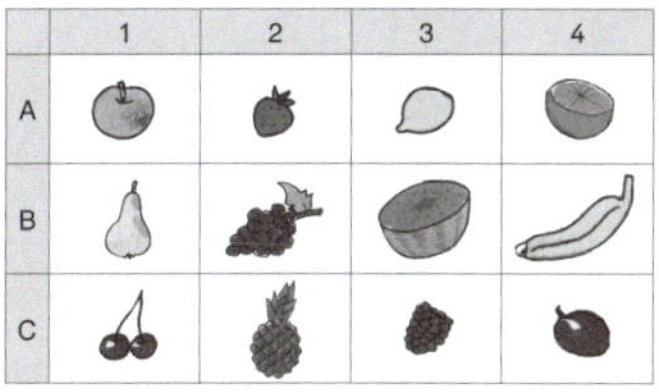

	1	2	3	4
A				
B				
C				

apple
banana
cherries
grapes
lemon
melon
orange
pear
pineapple
plum
strawberry
raspberry

A1 **apple**   B1 **pear**

B4 **banana**   C4 **plum**

C1 **cherries**   A4 **orange**

B2 **grapes**   C2 **pineapple**

A3 **lemon**   A2 **strawberry**

B3 **melon**   C3 **raspberry**

34

Page 35

Fruit

3. Look at the comic and write. ✓

Strawberries and **cherries** are red.

Apples and **pears** are green.

Lemons and **bananas** are yellow.

Plums are purple.

Oranges are orange.

Grapes are blue.

4. Correct or wrong?
Circle the letters and you will find a fruit. Draw it. ✓

	correct	wrong
Lucy likes to eat fruit.	P	(A)
Bananas are red.	L	(P)
Lemons are yellow.	(P)	U
Cherries are big.	M	(L)
Lucy eats a rainbow of fruit.	(E)	S

A P P L E

35

Page 36

Pets

Comic ?

All my pets

(comic illustrations with speech bubbles):

I have only got one dog. I'd like to have another dog and a budgie.

Make your wishes.

BLING!

I would also like to have a guinea pig, a mouse, a rabbit and a hamster.

I'm so happy. I have got lots of pets.

And I'd like to have a cat, and a fish, and a tortoise.

BLING!

Oh no!

Oh, good, it was only a dream. One pet is enough for me.

36

Page 37

Pets

1. What do you see in the squares? Look and write. ✓ ?

	1	2	3
A			
B			
C			

budgie   tortoise
fish   dog
rabbit   mouse
cat   hamster
guinea pig

B1: It's a **rabbit**.   A1: **It's a fish**.

C3: It's a **tortoise**.   C1: **It's a budgie**.

C2: **It's a guinea pig**.   B3: **It's a cat**.

A3: **It's a mouse**.   A2: **It's a hamster**.

B2: **It's a dog**.

2. Whose is it? Write. ✓

tortoise   **budgie**

dog   **hamster**

fish

cat

Zu welchem Tier gehört welcher Gegenstand? Schreibe auf.

37

Lösungen

3. Look at the comic. Number the pets in the correct order. ✓

7, 8, 6
4, 1, 5
3, 2, 9

4. Which animals are missing? Write. ✓

The **rabbit**, the **budgie**, the **fish** and the **hamster** are missing.

The **cat**, the **tortoise** and the **mouse** are missing.

38

Comic ?

Fun outside

Sally, it stopped raining! Please go and play outside.
Goodbye, Mum.
Goodbye, Sally.
Climbing a tree is great
SCRATCH!
Thank you, bird, for this nice feather.
I love catching frogs in the pond.
Oh no, SALLY!!!!
Hello, Mum, I love playing outside.
I'm picking some flowers for Mum.

39

1. Find the words and draw lines. ✓

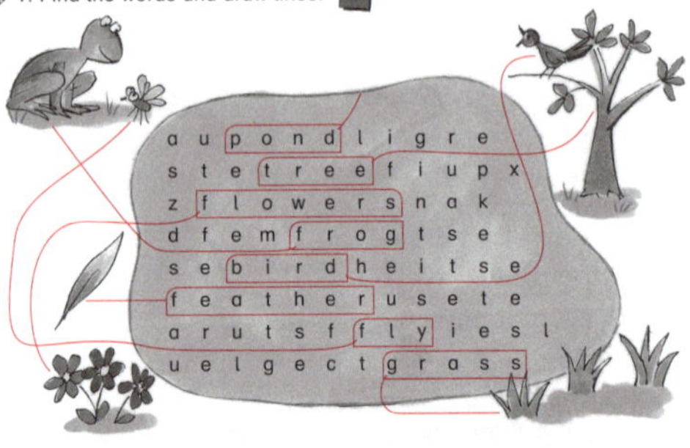

grass   pond   tree   fly   frog
feather   flowers   bird

2. Find out who it is. Look, read and write. ✓

Mary   **Andy**   **Lilly**   **Sam**

Andy is catching a **fly**.

Lilly is picking **flowers**.

Sam is climbing a **tree**.

Mary is jumping like a **frog**.

Vervollständige zunächst die Sätze. Ordne dann die Namen der Kinder dem passenden Bild zu.

40

3. Number the sentences in the correct order. Match them with the correct picture. ✓

Nummeriere die Sätze in der richtigen Reihenfolge und ordne sie dem passenden Bild zu.

4, 2
3

2 Sally has got a feather.

1 Sally is climbing a tree.

4 Sally is picking flowers for her mum.

3 Sally is catching a frog in the pond.

4. What does Sally like? Draw lines and circle the correct letter. Who's Sally's new friend? ✓

Sally likes catching frogs	in the pond. (f)
	in the grass. (b)
Sally likes picking flowers	for her sister. (i)
	for her mum. (r)
Sally likes climbing	a tree. (o)
	a house. (r)
Sally likes	colours. (d)
	feathers. (g)

Sally's new friend is a **frog**.

41

Comic ?

I want to ride a ...

42

1. Guess the farm animal. Write.

sheep · pig · horse · cow · duck · goose · hen

goose horse sheep
pig cow hen duck

2. What animal is it? Read and write.

It likes carrots and says neigh-neigh. It's a **horse**.

It's pink and says oink-oink. It's a **pig**.

It's big and gives milk. It's a **cow**.

It says cluck-cluck and lays eggs. It's a **hen**.

It can swim and says quak-quak. It's a **duck**.

It's bigger than a duck. It says honk-honk. It's a **goose**.

It eats grass and says baa-baa. It's a **sheep**.

43

3. Number the pictures in the correct order.

Achtung! Schau genau hin! Ein Bild musst du durchstreichen.

2, 3, 1

4. Correct or wrong? Tick.

	correct	wrong
The farmer is riding a pig.		✓
The boy wants to ride a cow.	✓	
The boy wants to feed a sheep.		✓
The boy wants to ride a goose.		✓
The hens, the ducks and the goose are laughing at the boy.	✓	

44

Comic ?

Hide-and-seek in London

45

Lösungen

1. Do the crossword.

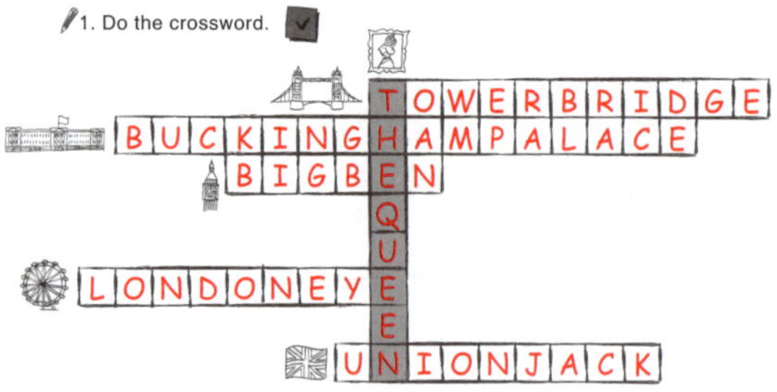

```
                        T O W E R B R I D G E
        B U C K I N G H A M P A L A C E
              B I G B E N
                        Q
                        U
    L O N D O N E Y     E
                        E
                    U N I O N J A C K
```

___The Queen___ lives at Buckingham Palace.

| Buckingham Palace | London Eye | Big Ben |
| Union Jack | the Queen | Tower Bridge |

2. Cross out.

~~The Union Jack~~ The London Eye is a big 🎡.

~~The London Eye~~ Big Ben is a 🔔.

Buckingham Palace ~~Tower Bridge~~ is the home of the 📮.

The Union Jack ~~Big Ben~~ is the 🇬🇧 of Great Britain.

46

3. Correct or wrong? Circle the letters and write down the word.

	correct	wrong
Sally and Koala are in New York.	C	(F)
Sally and Koala play hide-and-seek.	(L)	B
Sally and Koala visit the Queen.	N	(A)
Sally and Koala go by bus.	(G)	E

___FLAG___

4. Look and write.

Schau dir noch mal den Comic an. Schreibe auf, wer von beiden sich bei der abgebildeten Sehenswürdigkeit versteckt hat. Schreibe auch den Namen der Sehenswürdigkeit auf.

___Sally___ is on the ___London Eye___.

___Koala___ is at ___Buckingham Palace___.

___Koala___ is at ___Tower Bridge___.

47

Look at the comics again. Find the correct answer and write down the letter. What can you read?

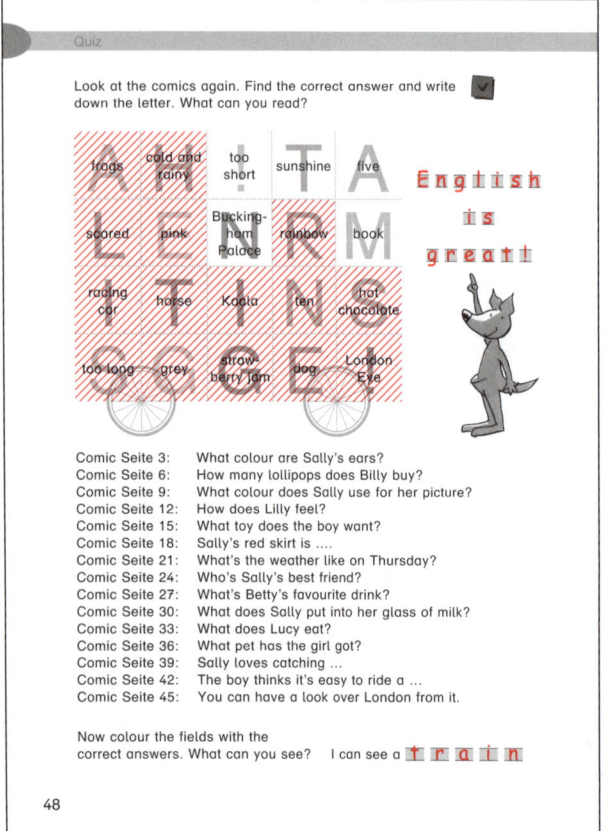

English is great!

frogs	cold and rainy	too short	sunshine	five
scored	pink	Buckingham Palace	rainbow	book
racing car	horse	Koala	ten	hot chocolate
too long	grey	strawberry jam	dog	London Eye

Comic Seite 3:   What colour are Sally's ears?
Comic Seite 6:   How many lollipops does Billy buy?
Comic Seite 9:   What colour does Sally use for her picture?
Comic Seite 12: How does Lilly feel?
Comic Seite 15: What toy does the boy want?
Comic Seite 18: Sally's red skirt is ....
Comic Seite 21: What's the weather like on Thursday?
Comic Seite 24: Who's Sally's best friend?
Comic Seite 27: What's Betty's favourite drink?
Comic Seite 30: What does Sally put into her glass of milk?
Comic Seite 33: What does Lucy eat?
Comic Seite 36: What pet has the girl got?
Comic Seite 39: Sally loves catching ...
Comic Seite 42: The boy thinks it's easy to ride a ...
Comic Seite 45: You can have a look over London from it.

Now colour the fields with the correct answers. What can you see?   I can see a **train**

48

✏ **1. Who is it? Write.** ✔

27601

27602

27603	27604	27605
t e m r o h	t h r r d n a a f e g	f a h r t e
_____	_____	_____

27606	27607	27608
r h b o r t e	m n e a g h r r t o d	e s s r i t
_____	_____	_____

27609	27610	27611
u a t n	u c n i o s	c e u l n
_____	_____	_____

✏ **2. Different families. Write.** ✔

27651

27652

Schau genau hin und ergänze dann die Sätze.

27653

I live with my father, my _____ and my _____.

27654

I live with my _____, my _____ and my _____.

27655

I live with my _____, my _____, my _____, my uncle, my _____ and my _____.

 3. Draw lines.

28101   28102

These are
my uncle, my aunt,
my cousin, my grandpa
and my grandma.

28103

Koala,
come to our pool
party.

28104

28107

Ordne die
Sprechblase
dem richtigen
Bild zu.

These are
my father, my mother,
my brother and
my sister.

28105

28108

And this is
my best friend
Koala.

28106

28109

28110

 4. Who is it? Read, look and write.

28151   28152

 Who is it? He's wearing green trousers.

28153

 That's my _____.

28157

 Who is it? She's wearing a pink dress.

28154

 That's my _____.

28158

 Who is it? He's wearing a yellow T-shirt.

28155

 That's my _____.

28159

 Who is it? She's wearing a purple skirt.

28156

 That's my _____.

28160

Schau dir
den Comic noch mal
genau an und
ergänze dann
die Sätze.

26

 Comic

28601   28651

A game with drinks
28602

Come on, let's play a game.

What is it, Jack?

28603

Ah, that's orange juice.

One is water and one is lemonade.

28604

Ew! That tastes bitter! That's coffee! Now it's your turn!

28605

28606

Yummy, it's my favourite drink, hot chocolate.

28607

Mmmm, one is milk. I like it. The other one is coke.

What is it, Betty?

Now you get my favourite drink.

8608

I'm mixing everything together.

28609

Do you like my special drink?

28610

28611

27

🖊 1. What is it? Write. ✅
29101
29102

29103

29104

29105

29106

29107

29108

29109

29110

29111

apple juice	milk	coke	lemonade	tea
29001	29002	29003	29004	29005
hot chocolate	**coffee**	**water**	**orange juice**	
29006	29007	29008	29009	

📕🖊 2. Read and write. ✅
29151
29152

It's cold, bubbly and made from lemons. It's _____.
29153

It's cold, brown and sweet. Children like it. It's _____.
29154

It's cold. It's made from apples. It's _____.
29155

You can drink it warm or cold. It's white and from a cow.
29156

It's _____.

It's hot, brown and sweet. You make it with milk.
29157

It's _____.

29158

3. Cross out. ✔

29601
29602

Jack likes | doesn't like coffee.

Coffee tastes bitter | sweet .

Betty likes | doesn't like milk.

Betty's favourite drink is coke | hot chocolate .

> Streiche jeweils die falsche Aussage durch.

4. Look at the comic and write. ✔

29651
29652

Jack

> Schreibe auf, welche Getränke Jack und welche Betty probiert hat.

29653

Betty

29654

What's your favourite drink?

My favourite drink is _____ .

Comic

30101

30151

Sally's special breakfast

30102

RiNGGG!

Oh, I'm sooooo tired.

Good morning, Mum.

30103

Good morning, Sally. Would you like milk, orange juice or tea? And would you like a roll with butter or bread with ham?

Just hot chocolate.

30104

30105

Oh, no! I put strawberry jam into the milk.

I'll try it.

30106

Yummy! It's strawberry-jam milk.

30107

Now, I'm ready for school!

30108

Goodbye, Mum. And thank you for the great breakfast.

Oh, Sally!

30109

30110

1. Find the words and draw lines.

30601

30602

Finde die Wörter, kreise sie ein und verbinde dann mit dem richtigen Bild.

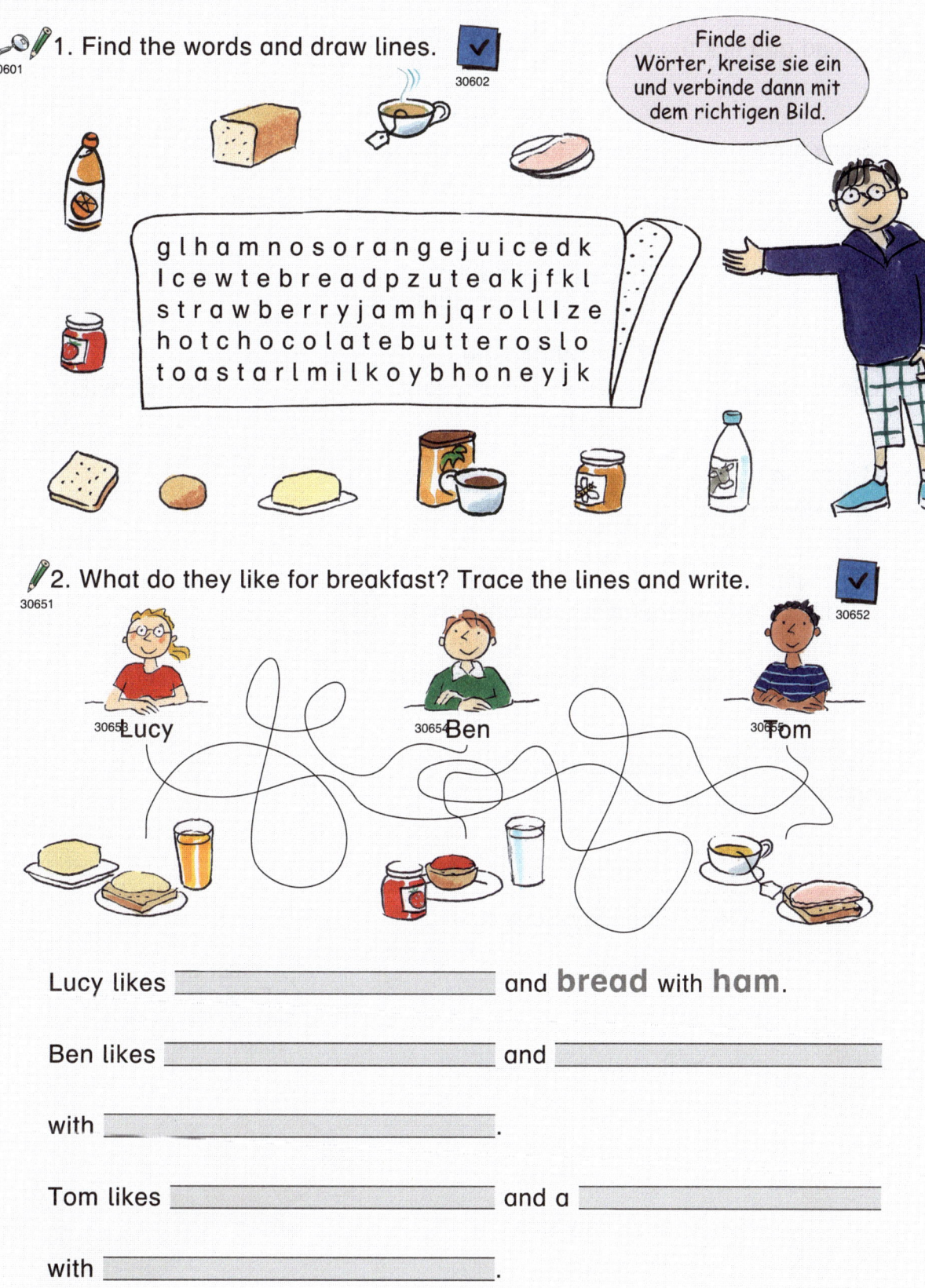

```
g l h a m n o s o r a n g e j u i c e d k
l c e w t e b r e a d p z u t e a k j f k l
s t r a w b e r r y j a m h j q r o l l l z e
h o t c h o c o l a t e b u t t e r o s l o
t o a s t a r l m i l k o y b h o n e y j k
```

2. What do they like for breakfast? Trace the lines and write.

30651

30652

30653 Lucy

30654 Ben

30655 Tom

Lucy likes _____ and **bread** with **ham**.

Ben likes _____ and _____

with _____ .

Tom likes _____ and a _____

with _____ .

3. Read and tick the correct answer.
31101
31102

Sally says:	Hello, Mum. ○ Good morning, Mum. ○ Good night, Mum. ○	
Sally wants ...	milk ○ orange juice ○ hot chocolate ○	for breakfast.
Sally puts ...	chocolate ○ strawberry jam ○ ham ○	into her milk.
Does Sally like strawberry milk?	Yes, she does. ○ No, she doesn't. ○	

4. Sally's crazy breakfast. Look and write.
31151
31152

On Monday Sally has strawberry-jam milk.

31153

On Tuesday Sally has an
orange-juice roll .
31154

On Wednesday Sally has
_____.
31155

On Thursday Sally has

_____.
31156

> But on Saturday and Sunday, there's no school – and I'm not tired.

On Friday Sally has
_____.
31157

31158

 Comic ❓

31601   31651

Eating a rainbow

31602

Lucy, eat some fruit. It's good for you.

I don't like to eat what's good for me.

31603

Strawberries are red – and cherries are red, too.

Oranges are orange.

31604

Lemons are yellow – and bananas are yellow, too.

31605

Apples are green – and pears are green, too.

31606

Well, grapes are blue.

31607

Plums are purple.

31608

Good girl, you're eating fruit.

I'm not eating fruit, Mummy, I'm eating a rainbow.

31609   31610

31611

33

✏ 1. Draw lines. ✓
32101   32102

raspberries
32103

oranges
32114

melons
32104

plums
32113

bananas
32105

lemons
32112

apples
32106

pineapples
32111

cherries
32107

pears
32110

grapes
32108

strawberries
32109

✏ 2. What can you see in the squares? Write. ✓ ?
32151   32152 32201

	1	2	3	4
A	 32153	 32154	 32155	 32156
B	 32157	 32158	 32159	 32160
C	 32161	 32162	 32163	 32164

apple
32001
banana
32002
cherries
32003
grapes
32004
lemon
32005
melon
32006
orange
32007
pear
32008
pineapple
32009
plum
32010
strawberry
32011
raspberry
32012

A1 ▢▢▢▢▢   B1 ▢▢▢▢

B4 ▢▢▢▢▢▢   C4 ▢▢▢▢

C1 ▢▢▢▢▢▢▢▢   A4 ▢▢▢▢▢▢

B2 ▢▢▢▢▢▢   C2 ▢▢▢▢▢▢▢▢▢

A3 ▢▢▢▢▢   A2 ▢▢▢▢▢▢▢▢▢▢

B3 ▢▢▢▢▢   C3 ▢▢▢▢▢▢▢▢▢

3. Look at the comic and write. ☑

32601

32602

_____ and _____ are red.

_____ and _____ are green.

_____ and _____ are yellow.

_____ are purple.

_____ are orange.

_____ are blue.

4. Correct or wrong?
Circle the letters and you will find a fruit. Draw it. ☑

32603

32604

	correct	wrong
Lucy likes to eat fruit. 32605	P	A
Bananas are red. 32606	L	P
Lemons are yellow. 32607	P	U
Cherries are big. 32608	M	L
Lucy eats a rainbow of fruit. 32609	E	S

▬ ▬ ▬ ▬ ▬

📕 Comic ❓

33101   33151

All my pets

33102

33103

33104

BLING!

33165

BLING!

I would also like to have a guinea pig, a mouse, a rabbit and a hamster.

BLING! 33162 BLING!

33163

33164

BLING!

33161

I'm so happy. I have got lots of pets.

33105   33160

33106

And I'd like to have a cat, and a fish, and a tortoise.

BLING!

BLING!

33107

I have only got one dog. I'd like to have another dog and a budgie.

Make your wishes.

33108

Oh no!

33109

Oh, good, it was only a dream. One pet is enough for me.

1. What do you see in the squares? Look and write.

33601

	1	2	3
A	33603	33604	33605
B	33606	33607	33608
C	33609	33610	33611

budgie
33501

tortoise
33502

fish
33503

dog
33504

rabbit
33505

mouse
33506

cat
33507

hamster
33508

guinea pig
33509

B1: It's a _____. A1: _____.

C3: It's a _____. C1: _____.

C2: _____. B3: _____.

A3: _____. A2: _____.

B2: _____.

2. Whose is it? Write.

33701

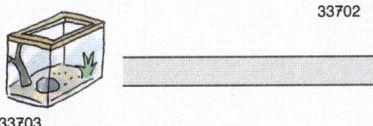 33703 _____

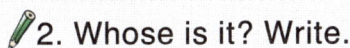 33704 _____

33705 _____

33706 _____

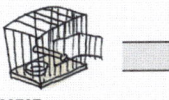 33707 _____

 33708 _____

Zu welchem Tier gehört welcher Gegenstand? Schreibe auf.

37

3. Look at the comic. Number the pets in the correct order. ✔

34101

34102

4. Which animals are missing? Write. ✔

34151

34152

34153

The _____, the

_____, the _____

and the _____ are missing.

34154

The _____, the

_____ and the

_____ are missing.

38

🔖 **Comic** ❓

34601   34651

Fun outside

34602

1. Find the words and draw lines. ✓
35101   35102

```
a u p o n d l i g r e
s t e t r e e f i u p x
z f l o w e r s n a k
d f e m f r o g t s e
s e b i r d h e i t s e
f e a t h e r u s e t e
a r u t s f f l y i e s l
u e l g e c t g r a s s
```

grass	pond	tree	fly	frog
35001	35002	35003	35004	35005
	feather	flowers	bird	
	35006	35007	35008	

2. Find out who it is. Look, read and write. ✓
35151   35152

35153    35154    35155    35156

Andy is catching a _____.

Lilly is picking _____.

Sam is climbing a _____.

Mary is jumping like a _____.

Ver-
vollständige
zunächst die
Sätze. Ordne dann
die Namen der
Kinder dem
passenden
Bild zu.

40

123 3. **Number the sentences in the correct order.**
   Match them with the correct picture.

35601   35602

Nummeriere die Sätze in der richtigen Reihenfolge und ordne sie dem passenden Bild zu.

Sally has got a feather.
35603

Sally is climbing a tree.
35604

Sally is picking flowers for her mum.
35605

Sally is catching a frog in the pond.
35606

4. **What does Sally like? Draw lines and circle the correct letter.**
   Who's Sally's new friend?

35651   35652

Sally likes catching frogs	in the pond. (f) in the grass. (b)
Sally likes picking flowers	for her sister. (i) for her mum. (r)
Sally likes climbing	a tree. (o) a house. (r)
Sally likes	colours. (d) feathers. (g)

Sally's new friend is a _____ .

Comic

36101 36151

I want to ride a …

36102

36103

36104

36105

36106

36107

36109

36111

36110

1. Guess the farm animal. Write. ✔

36601

36602

36603

36604

36605

goose	horse	sheep
36501 36502 36503
pig	cow	hen	duck
36504 36505 36506 36507

36606

36607

36608

36609

2. What animal is it? Read and write. ✔

36651

36652

It likes carrots and says neigh-neigh. It's a ▢▢▢▢▢ .
36653

It's pink and says oink-oink. It's a ▢▢▢ .
36654

It's big and gives milk. It's a ▢▢▢ .
36655

It says cluck-cluck and lays eggs. It's a ▢▢▢ .
36656

It can swim and says quak-quak. It's a ▢▢▢▢ .
36657

It's bigger than a duck. It says honk-honk. It's a ▢▢▢▢▢ .
36658

It eats grass and says baa-baa. It's a ▢▢▢▢▢ .
36659

3. Number the pictures in the correct order.

37101

37102

Achtung!
Schau genau hin!
Ein Bild musst du
durchstreichen.

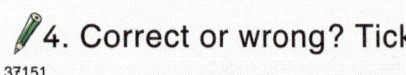 **4. Correct or wrong? Tick.**

37151

37152

	correct	wrong
The farmer is riding a pig. 37153	○	○
The boy wants to ride a cow. 37154	○	○
The boy wants to feed a sheep. 37155	○	○
The boy wants to ride a goose. 37156	○	○
The hens, the ducks and the goose are laughing at the boy. 37157	○	○

44

 Comic

37601

37651

Hide-and-seek in London

37602

I love London.

Now, what are we going to do?

I've got an idea, let's play hide-and-seek.

WELCOME TO LONDON

37603

37604

Got you! You're at Big Ben.

37605   37606

37607

Got you! You're on the London Eye.

Got you! You're at Buckingham Palace.

37609

37608

37610

London is fantastic.

VISIT LONDON

37611

37612

Got you! You're at Tower Bridge.

37613

45

1. Do the crossword.

38101   38102   38103

38104

38105

38106

38107

38108

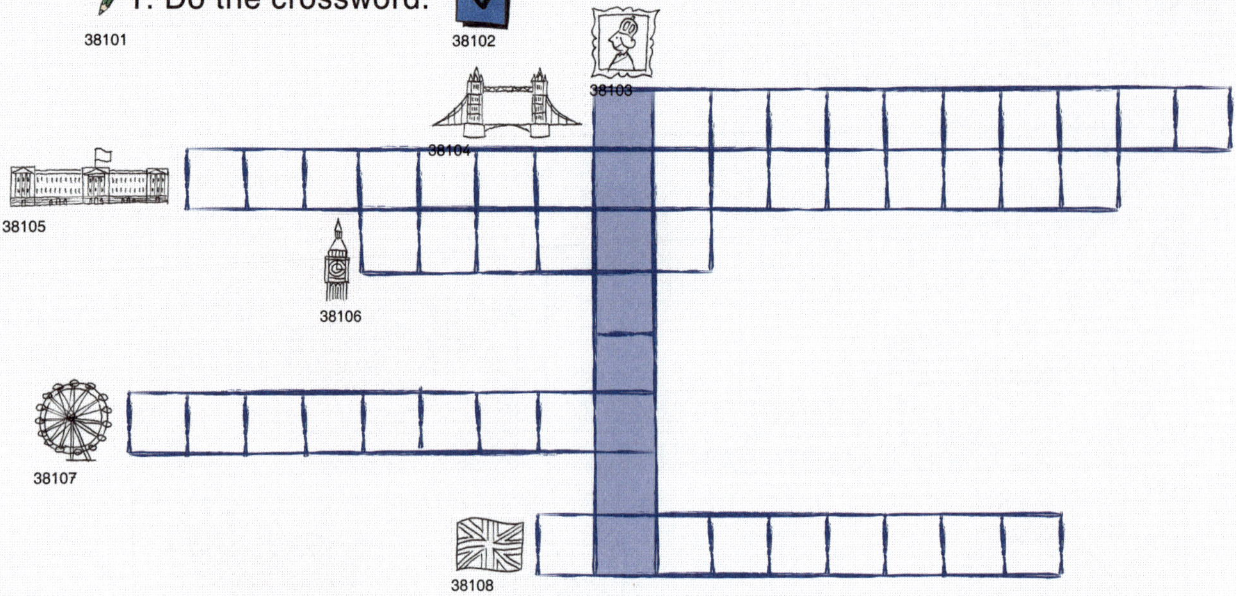

_____ lives at Buckingham Palace.

Buckingham Palace 38001	**London Eye** 38002	**Big Ben** 38003
Union Jack 38004	**the Queen** 38005	**Tower Bridge** 38006

2. Cross out.

38151   38152

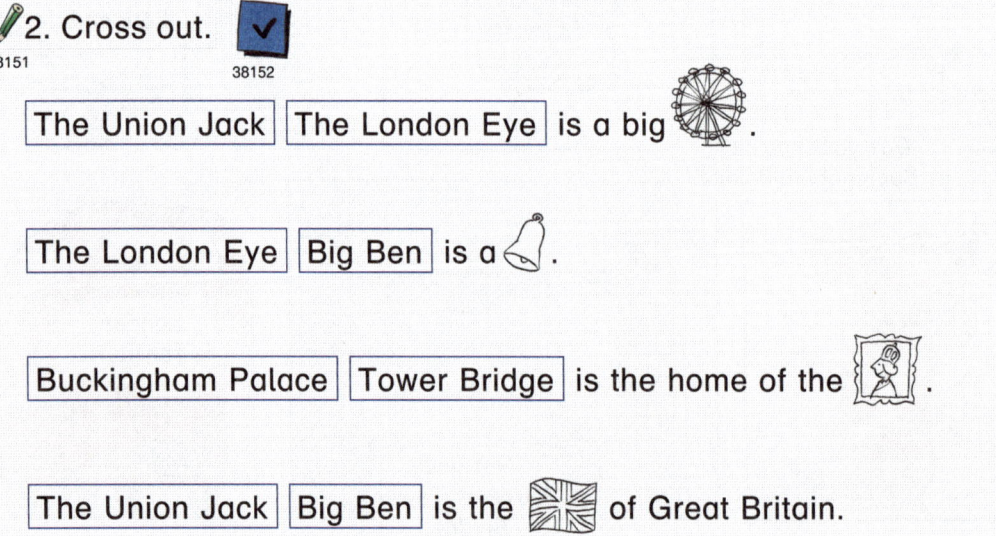

| The Union Jack | The London Eye | is a big ⚙ .

| The London Eye | Big Ben | is a 🔔 .

| Buckingham Palace | Tower Bridge | is the home of the 🖼 .

| The Union Jack | Big Ben | is the 🏴 of Great Britain.

46

3. Correct or wrong? Circle the letters and write down the word.

38601

38602

	correct	wrong
Sally and Koala are in New York. 38603	C	F
Sally and Koala play hide-and-seek. 38604	L	B
Sally and Koala visit the Queen. 38605	N	A
Sally and Koala go by bus. 38606	G	E

_____

38607

 4. Look and write.

38651

38652

38653

_____ is on the _____.

38654

_____ is at _____.

38655

_____ is at _____.

Schau dir noch mal den Comic an. Schreibe auf, wer von beiden sich bei der abgebildeten Sehenswürdigkeit versteckt hat. Schreibe auch den Namen der Sehenswürdigkeit auf.

Look at the comics again. Find the correct answer and write down the letter. What can you read?
39139

39101

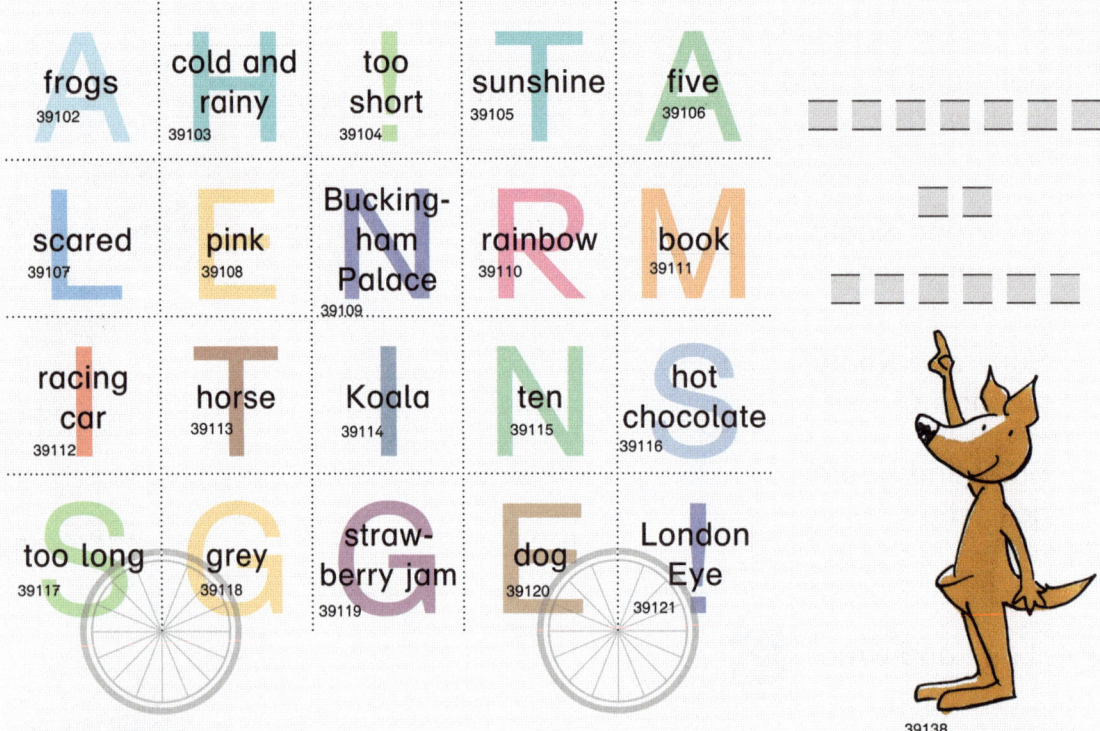

A frogs 39102	H cold and rainy 39103	T too short 39104	A sunshine 39105	A five 39106
L scared 39107	E pink 39108	N Bucking-ham Palace 39109	R rainbow 39110	M book 39111
I racing car 39112	T horse 39113	I Koala 39114	N ten 39115	S hot chocolate 39116
S too long 39117	G grey 39118	E straw-berry jam 39119	G dog 39120	! London Eye 39121

39138

Comic Seite 3:   What colour are Sally's ears?
Comic Seite 6:   How many lollipops does Billy buy? 39122
Comic Seite 9:   What colour does Sally use for her picture? 39123
Comic Seite 12:   How does Lilly feel? 39124
Comic Seite 15:   What toy does the boy want? 39125
Comic Seite 18:   Sally's red skirt is …. 39126
Comic Seite 21:   What's the weather like on Thursday? 39127
Comic Seite 24:   Who's Sally's best friend? 39128
Comic Seite 27:   What's Betty's favourite drink? 39129
Comic Seite 30:   What does Sally put into her glass of milk? 39130
Comic Seite 33:   What does Lucy eat? 39131
Comic Seite 36:   What pet has the girl got? 39132
Comic Seite 39:   Sally loves catching … 39133
Comic Seite 42:   The boy thinks it's easy to ride a … 39134
Comic Seite 45:   You can have a look over London from it. 39135
39136

Now colour the fields with the correct answers. What can you see?   I can see a ▢▢▢▢▢▢
39137

48